# Let's Get Rich, *QUICK*!

Copyright © 2019 by Emmett Ferguson

All rights reserved. No portion of this book may be reproduced, stored in a retrieval system, or transmitted in any form or by any means-electronic, mechanical, photocopy, recording, scanning or other-except for brief quotations in critical reviews or articles, without the prior written permission from the Publisher.

Published by Strategic Possibilities Consulting
Cover Designed by Melissa Discepolo

**ISBN:** 9781670164551

This book has opinions and ideas of the author. It is intended to give helpful and informative material on the subjects addressed in the publication. It is sold with the understanding that the author –and publisher are not engaged in giving professional tax and or legal advice or any other kind of personal or professional services in the book.

The reader should consult his or her consultants, tax and financial advisor, attorney or other competent professional before adopting any of the concepts in this book or drawing inferences from it. The content of this book, by its very nature, is general. Meanwhile, each reader's situation is unique. Therefore, as with all books of this nature, the purpose is to give general information rather than address individual situations, which books by their very nature cannot do.

The author and publisher specifically disclaim all responsibility for any liability, loss, or risk, personal or otherwise, which is incurred consequently, directly or indirectly, of the use and application of any of the contents of this book.

*Thanks to Lisa Narh,
Matt Hirschberg, and
Jordan Belfort for
inviting me into the
company that inspired this book.*

# Contents

| | | |
|---|---|---|
| Introduction | | 5 |
| 1. | Dear Reader | 10 |
| 2. | First Things First | 13 |
| 3. | Reasons to Get Rich | 17 |
| 4. | Right People in Your Life | 24 |
| 5. | No Secrets Here | 30 |
| 6. | Seek Success | 36 |
| 7. | Like Yourself | 40 |
| 8. | Advance, Not Stagnate | 43 |
| 9. | Why Money? | 47 |
| 10. | Let's Do Mathematics | 53 |
| 11. | Say No to Mediocre | 59 |
| 12. | Get Inspired | 65 |
| 13. | Spread the Wealth | 70 |
| Conclusion | | 74 |
| About the Author | | 75 |

# Introduction

Do you want to get rich? Let's do it together! How many people have you ever had in your life that want you to find massive success and riches in your life?

Do you even want it for yourself? Do you think your boss, your neighbor, or coworker, deeply wants you to see you get rich? Does your teacher, life coach, parent, sister want you to get rich? Or do they hope that you succeed and wish you the best? Have you ever even had the "how do we get rich (with integrity)" conversation in depth with a *serious* group of people?

The thought of getting rich can deter many people from even getting started on the journey. Think about it for a moment. It is scary to talk about… Money. $$$

Even the thought of rounding up a fast-food bill by $0.28 to donate to a charity can cause someone to automatically trigger the automatic defensive wall response of "no."

The mere thought of getting rich, and all the beliefs around getting rich, the challenges and fears of what it means to become rich can cause someone to stop the pursuit of riches before they even put any action behind it. And therefore, miss out on the experience of becoming rich.

Even the rich perpetuate some of these negative beliefs themselves when they become "unhappy." An obvious example is wealthy Hollywood studios in the film industry producing Hollywood box office films, painting the rich as greedy and evil. Irony.

At the same time, there are many people who only think about becoming rich day in and day out but fail to realize it in the physical world in the amount of time they hoped. Every day there is a new social media advertisement telling you about how you can make money with this one new method or marketing tactic.

And others are born into money – fair enough. You know what they say: "the best way to get rich is to be born rich." When life hands you money, do something with it!

But *Let's Get Rich, QUICK!* is not about "how to get rich," although there are a handful of ideas presented in this book that may help you get to where you want to go, effectively, based on research. Nor is it even about a new popular self-help coaching concept that is dedicated to helping you perform more effectively in your job and life so that eventually, your purpose and habits transform you into a wealthy individual.

(And we all know when popular books say wealthy, they rarely ever mean money-wise. They often define wealthy as areas of life such as happiness, spirituality, health, family, friends, a purpose, and a "living a fulfilled life.")

As important as personal development and living a life with the right integrity and purpose is, spending your life doing things you are "passionate about" can keep you unhappy.

Are starving artists truly happy? They live in the future of what they hope life can be, and most fail to succeed.

But I love the arts, and this is not to disparage artists or the pursuit of dreams. The goal is to put the ideas in this book in front of you, to get you inspired to get rich so that you can do whatever it is you want and love in the future because you can (and also because you're talented)!

If you are rich already, you probably don't need this book to find what you are looking for. If you are rich already (and what you seek is beyond money), go find a great seminar and work on a greater purpose, seek personal development, tackle a new physical fitness journey, go on a spiritual awakening in Tibet, have a sabbatical to focus on family, or jump into a new business or investment.

This book is for those who have the massive desire to get to a place of financial success when they have no one else around them that cares as much as they do.

This book is for those who are ready to stop beating around the bush and focus on the fact that you want to get rich. Maybe you have a purpose already and are tired of the same "here are what the most successful people in the world do, follow these actions, and you might get there *(eventually)*" advice.

*Let's Get Rich, QUICK!* is also not about how to save money or whether real estate, stocks, or entrepreneurship is a better way to success than working your way to the top. It doesn't matter how you do it; just get to it!

*Let's Get Rich, QUICK!* is also not about those same ideas that financial companies are touting about residual income, and saving money, so that sometime in 40 years from now, when the compound interest from some investments might make you a millionaire (if everything goes perfectly) in your middle to high five-figure, or even low six-figure job.

There are no fancy equations, and having a good team of smart financial experts, accountants, and money managers around you is hugely important in making sure your money grows, but you have to get there and be able to afford them first!

With all that said about what this book is not about, the question remains unanswered:

What is *Let's Get Rich, QUICK!* about? Let me ask you this.

When was the last time anyone said to you, "I want you to get rich?" Or "Hey friend, let's get incredibly rich, now how do we get there?" And meant it?

Think about that for a moment.

Who was the last person you had in your life (even as a symbol or someone you looked up to) who deeply wanted you to get rich?

And what is the power of having people in your life like that? Sure, "no one can do your push-ups for you" as the renown personal development expert Jim Rohn once said, and there is something to be said about self-reliance, but not one single person on earth becomes massively wealthy, rich, and successful on their own.

And that is ultimately what this book is about: getting together on that one spark in your life that is going to get you to where you want to go: RICH!

So how does this book matter if it is not a "how-to?" There are researched and studied ideas that are going to help you on your journey. Some of the ideas are interpretations and conclusions I have drawn based on observations. Let's get you taking on bigger actions in your life through a combination of helping you, to evaluate what it means to get rich, what resources are out there to help you, and what it is you can do about getting yourself rich.

# 1. Dear Reader

This book and its' ideas do not care where you've been, nor where you want to go. The main focus is to discuss the seemingly taboo subject of getting rich.

Whether you are:
A veteran finishing your first contract…
A non-profit worker, teacher, entry-level employee, or college student working three jobs…
An artist looking to get discovered…
A doctor, lawyer, or other professional that requires extensive educational background…
A small business owner…
A craftsman of some sort…
From a tough neighborhood…
Are struggling to figure out what you want to do with your life, or know what you want to do but just haven't gotten there yet…
Unable or unqualified (on paper) to get the job you want or work at the company you want…
Not networked enough to get big contracts…

This book is for you. This book is for anyone who has a desire to make a lot of money. It is for you to have a resource, a symbol of something that equates to the energy that wants you to get rich. Quite frankly, if you have never had the conversation about getting rich, or you've thought about it but never had anyone wish it for you, this book will help you.

I wrote *Let's Get Rich, QUICK!* because there is so much information out there that avoids talking about the simple topic of being able to afford anything you could want and make more income than you can easily spend. I am not saying those books are not valuable. I am, however, saying that there is a missing conversation in the world of becoming successful. The how-tos are out there, but the conversation is much rarer.

If no one has ever told you they want you to get rich, or you cannot name more than five people close to you who you feel aim incredibly high in a financial sense, this book is for you because those might be the simple things that are holding you back! Imagine wanting to go out to a party, but either no one wants to go with you or all your friends prefer to stay at home.

Or imagine wanting to build a company or get into shape, but not knowing of anyone around you who knows how to build a company, and the people around you aren't motivated to get into shape. Much more difficult to accomplish anything isn't it? The conversations in this book will help you overcome those challenges.

Most broke people justify being broke by saying "money doesn't buy happiness" or "money can't solve all your problems. But I argue that it is acceptable to feel that money can help solve some problems because whether you are rich or not, there will always be problems to solve.

The ideas in this book have been researched and developed after endless numbers of articles, books, courses, seminars, and more. You may not get rich simply by owning this book, and no one out there (who has built a long term reputation for helping people find success) will take the risk of promising they can make people rich, and neither can I. But I write to you to help you get a conversation started!

# 2. First Things First

Do you want long-lasting success? Do you want generational riches? Do you want enough money that will allow you to do as much as you want and still have more than you can easily spend on a day to day basis?

Or do you want to have to watch your back every day? Trying to keep all your wealth a secret… Or even working hard, and experiencing the life of a rich man or woman, but fearing that in 20 years or less, that it might ALL get taken away? Of course not!

The most important idea to gain from all these questions is the concept of integrity. If you are smart and ambitious enough to get rich or successful via unscrupulous business practices or less than ethical activities, you are probably smart enough to become rich doing ethical work as well. This section is not meant to judge the work anyone does, as much as it is to establish that there are many ways to make great money that allows you to sleep better and enjoy more life!

Aim to create long-lasting wealth. Not something that the courts will have a great reason to take away from you in a few years from now. And this book was not written to judge what you do with your money either.

If you get rich, only to lose it all spending it frivolously and not being able to make it back, at least you had the opportunity to get there! But think about the possibilities here. The full potential of the energy of money.

A lot of the stigma around rich people is often wrong, and I attribute it to this simple fact: there are many unhappy rich people just like there are multiples of other unhappy broke people. But the simple desire to become massively successful only breeds more great products, brands, companies, technologies, and more!

Money allows the creative to become even more creative because they can afford to find solace between their creations. Sure, the sense of urgency from poverty can too.

Money allows the entrepreneur to try new ideas in the case of serial entrepreneurship or continue growing and expanding their current idea. Money allows the socialite to continue traveling the world and continue expanding their network and living the life most dream about and follow. Money allows the poor to get out of the state they live in and find opportunities. Money allows for technology, experiences, medicines, and more.

There is much to love about money when it is applied beneficially to society and life. Not necessarily for money alone, but what it can potentially bring into our lives. Why not pursue it?

Many respected thought leaders mention that you need to figure out "why" you want to get rich in the first place, or you have to find a niche, or you have to invest right, or you have to buy into some new training program, or you have to figure out what you are really good at and maximize your potential through that and eventually you might get rich. But you can go broke doing all those things too.

I want you to get rich so you can be like those guys that legends are made of! And the legends that make history know how to keep their money growing with calculated, ethical risks.

By trying to get rich without integrity or the right ethics, you will be battling yourself every day. Eventually, you may get "numb" to what you are doing, whether that be betraying, scamming, or trying to constantly hide things from people. But what if all that energy spent trying to "cover-up" was applied in a way that was much more beneficial to people? Much more could be achieved.

Why take a path of so much resistance? There are enough stories of failure and fall from grace figures who were sent to prison for their issues. There are also enough stories of the pain of getting money without feeling deserving of it. Ideally, you will deserve every cent of your riches.

The other "first thing" other people might be wondering is who the heck is the author? Is he qualified? Is he rich? How did he make his money? Does he just want to sell me this book without adding any new or innovative ideas? Is he another motivational speaker? How long has he been around for? What are his handles on social media?

At the time of writing this book, I am ambitious for riches just like you. I grew up doing busboy and server work in restaurants, worked in water parks, and although I worked hard, I never really understood money. I valued it, but did not understand it.

I just knew I wanted money and success but cannot say I worked effectively at getting it. Working in a restaurant is not working effectively to get rich. I even had many negative beliefs and assumptions about what money means. But I was also taught some great things about money, such as how to manage it. I would say I earned the right to learn the value of the dollar from the work I did. But before going more into detail about myself.

Let's take this moment to decide to learn from the mistakes of others, and let's continue…

# 3. Reasons to Get Rich

Fear and lack of knowledge about the markets. Billions if not trillions of dollars sitting in banks waiting for the right idea or investment. Financially challenged millennials. Rich people pay thousands of dollars to high-end coaches that help them perform better (and mostly to help themselves first).

Endless advertisements about every opportunity out there from franchises to entrepreneurship, to work at home opportunities with low barriers to entry and streaming video games to make money. The need to be a writer, marketer, video producer, personable on camera, leader, and can deliver compelling speeches to an audience to compete.

There is no lack of "purpose" that comes with a desire to get rich. Providing more for a family is a purpose. Giving more back to the community is a purpose. Buying a sports team is a purpose. Feeding a healthy ego is a purpose.

Writers, motivational speakers, and social success theorists can go down an endless conversation helping their clients find a purpose in their life. And in theory, by finding one's purposes or reasons for living, one can become "wealthy."

Why not make your purpose getting rich and making, having, and investing a ton of money? Along that route, you may also find another purpose you are passionate about, such as finger painting or the construction of skyscrapers, or something more philanthropic like being on the board of a non-profit organization.

The rich and successful love to tell the ambitious about finding your brand and developing your voice and not being scared to take risk. But how many people are telling you to get rich? Is it that frightening and wrong? And if getting rich does frighten you, and you believe it is wrong, riches may most certainly be harder to come by. Let's eliminate those thoughts! Decide for yourself to get rich before moving onto the next sentence even!

I've invested much in education, personal development (aka self-help) and personal finance books. I've traveled, read, wrote, tested, and have numerous moments where I was unhappy with the results I've achieved. But I've also had the opportunity to earn a good amount of money, feel a level of comfort, and do some cool stuff while meeting great people along the way.

But regardless of the journey, while I've wanted to "be rich" I rarely ever focused on it, mainly because all the "thought leaders" say to focus on something like a purpose instead. The idea is that if you focus on everything except the assumedly "shallow idea" of getting rich, you will somehow get to where you want to go.

Although focusing on things other than money is a valuable feel-good concept that gets people engaged in conversation on social media, I feel it is to some degree, simply "accepting that you are not where you want to be financially," thereby justifying your position. That may not always be the case, but in many times, I think it is. This method of getting rich may even be completely avoidant, and even passive-aggressive to some level. That is, at least until you become rich.

You can spend 5 years doing many things: saving up for that dream car, putting a down payment on that new house, getting rich, becoming happy, finding that boyfriend or girlfriend, preparing for a child, saving for a child's college, writing that book or movie screenplay, networking. I don't believe getting rich is any better or worse than any other endeavor.

Money does not need to be a taboo subject (at least not while you're reading this book). Let your thoughts and dreams about money run wild. And to understand money, it is important to know how money and the concept of getting rich affect us emotionally.

If you are not rich, finding your purpose can be difficult. Especially when you are working multiple jobs, and trying to get out of debt, finding happiness and purpose can be difficult when you are broke.

It can be difficult to get confident when you have no money to date the woman of your dreams, and even though the mantra "if she only cares about money, blah blah blah" feels good, the reality is, part of you wants to be able to provide for the people you want to care about. And if the relationship ends, you'll want the opportunity to bounce back because you can provide for those you care about.

Now, this does not mean that emotional states only come from money. If you derive too much meaning in life from money, you can put yourself into a lot of trouble. We are often too emotionally attached to money, and that is what often causes us trouble.

The mere discussion of money can cause discomfort in us, and that is reasonable. Although it is important to manage our expectations about money, it is equally important to understand our emotions tied to it. The mere title, *Let's Get Rich, QUICK!* will likely bring about angry critics and enthusiastic readers!

*Let's Get Rich, QUICK!* so you can pursue that woman of your dreams. Get rich so you can save the planet, get the respect you feel you deserve and buy your island. Get rich so you can create a business that lasts for generations.

Get rich so you can throw massive yacht and penthouse parties and mingle with the rich and beautiful. Get rich so you can make decisions that matter. Get rich so you can sit around in a log cabin somewhere and write or read a book.

Get rich, so you can travel the world in a jet lined with gold, have a personal limo driver, security guards, and the latest technologies to keep you connected with your friends. Get rich so you can spend extra hours in meditation and physical fitness.

Get rich so you can play video games for the rest of your life or review new gadgets or do whacky stunts on video. Get rich so you can raise the best family. Get rich so you can give back to your community, religious organization, or favorite charitable cause.

And because money and acquiring a lot of it can provide all this opportunity and more, it is important to manage what it means to us. If you get rich, you might even find unhappiness and sorrow just as the poor or middle class might find unhappiness and sorrow.

Is a man or woman whose sole purpose in life was to get rich, and does so with integrity and the right ethics, any better or worse than the man or woman who dedicated their lives to mastering a sport or craft? The athlete and craftsman could have gotten rich along the way, but notice that getting rich can be a purpose too!

Maybe you have a sports coach that wants you to get better with your swing, and parent who wants you to do better on your grades. But who do you know that wants you to get rich?

Your parents probably haven't even thought about deeply wanting you to get rich. Not because they don't have high hopes for you, but because they are not sure how it is even possible, and also they are too focused on making sure you are safe and comfortable by following a traditional path.

When you have someone who believes in you to succeed in school, sports, business, family, or even spiritually, chances are you will go further. And QUICK is better than 50 years from now.

Maybe you are more internally or self-motivated and constantly compete with yourself. That is a good quality to have, but to get rich, you have to have someone who wants you to get there too.

And to have people that want you to get there, you either have to find something inspirational like this book. Or be in a position where you are adding tremendous value to the lives of many people, so much value that they will want nothing but the best for you and will buy your products and be happy that you or your company or salespeople are earning their money.

Many books will tell you about some of the ways to get rich, albeit very slowly and conservatively in many of them. But the simple act of having a token that represents your massive desire to become fascinatingly rich can cause a paradigm shift in you.

There are plenty of reasons to get rich. Manage those reasons for yourself. Get rich on your terms, for your own reasons. Money is important, but don't let it own you — own money.

Develop the desire for it, not just for the sake of having it, and if that is the case, so be it, but get rich because of all the things you know you can do when you reach a high level of financial success.

# 4. Right People in Your Life

Why do companies spend so much money on figuring out employee compensation plans, how to manage turnover, how to hire right, how to negotiate salaries, and how to keep employees engaged?

Why is there so much talk about why it is so important to be inclusive, have a great work atmosphere, develop collaboration, and hearing the opinions of everyone in the company?

Why is so much time spent politicking, working over our insecurities, and beating around the bush in business conversations?

Well, the obvious reason is that these things are important in work and society! They create more joy in our lives and more functional and collaborative groups.

Companies must understand how to manage people, find the right people, keep them, and continue developing future leaders in their organizations. As individuals, we also love to be recognized, feel challenged, and ideally enjoy the countless hours we spend at work. People will stay when they love the work they do!

But here's the thing people might not discuss. Many people and employees also want to get rich! But that's where the buck stops for most people, just "wanting" or "thinking about it."

People inherently have a desire to be greater, gain recognition, and pursue all their passions, and live life to the fullest potential, and to do that, money is a necessity.

Money is energy. Money is resources. Money is power, opportunity, and connections. If you think of "money is power" with a negative connotation, that might prevent you from getting you where you want to go. Power and the ability to influence can be a positive thing if used appropriately.

But here is the other part of all of this. So much time and resources are spent on the previously mentioned business challenges because managers need to figure out how to get more done while also keeping down expenses!

Companies can't afford to pay everyone an executive salary. They need to figure out how to keep employees engaged and still able to afford a living, even in places where the cost of living is exorbitant. And the engineer who spent 30+ years learning, maintaining, and developing new technology within a company surely deserves to earn more than the entry-level worker. Not everyone in a company can get rich on the company's dollar. And not everyone wants to get rich badly enough!

You can give the example of those highly respected men and women who were not money-driven and added tremendous value to the world like Gandhi, Mother Theresa, the Dalai Lama, and/or Martin Luther King, Jr. But you are none of those people, and unless you choose to become something like them, they may not be the best person to compare yourself to. If you wish to become a monk who gave up everything, then reading a book about getting rich may not be for you – and you might even find that you want to become a monk after you become rich!

If you prefer to pursue a life of spiritual, social change, and/or philanthropic giving without any interest in financial pursuit, more power to you. I hope you succeed in relieving the world of social challenges. There is still much to relieve with the right allocation of financial resources. Did you know many non-profit organizations still have executives that earn salaries that can make them rich?

And here is the thing about those success stories who did not necessarily aim to get rich, and part of that has to do with what *Let's Get Rich, QUICK!* is about: they all had people around them that wanted them to succeed! People with money and resources – and their agendas. People who had people around them who also wanted to get rich and get successful!

You see, it is crucial to have people in your life that want you to succeed. Of course, you have to desire it badly enough for yourself because external motivation can only take you so far. But external motivation, whether in the form of a muse, serendipity, or even a flash of an idea that excites you into competition is still a part of what keeps people inspired to achieve.

On the other hand, we know your boss, neighbor, high school friends, and co-workers could care less about whether you get massively rich or not. But what about the personal development experts and everyone writing books or delivering seminars about getting rich? While I believe a handful of them have great intentions, I would say most of them miss the mark on what many people seek their counsel for, to get rich.

If you want to get rich in finance, seek a banker or investment advisor. If you want to get rich in the automotive business, seek the owner of a dealership. If you want to get rich as an engineer, seek a degree or read books. If you want to get rich in helping others find success, research personal development. If you want to get rich feeding the world, learn about farming.

If you were not born rich, you'll have to work hard to earn it (or get incredibly lucky). If you were not born rich, you could also likely have more negative influences than positive ones as it relates to getting rich.

I'd have to say I was born in a state of fiscal neutrality. Not necessarily "middle class" because that is a demographic based on financial. But in terms of the overall beliefs about what it means to be rich, or what the possibilities are. I didn't have friends or mentors around me that inspired me to find wealth! And I didn't seek them either, so that is largely my fault. I had grains of desire, but not necessarily the burning desire you must develop to get where you want to go.

Finding money to get rich is not difficult. There is plenty at your local bank. There is *plenty* of money in the world. There may not be enough money for everyone to be a trillionaire, but for the people with the right ideas, integrity, action, and level of desire, money is available.

The difficult task for becoming rich is having people around you that want to do it with you, together, mainly because you, myself, and everyone else is selfish. That is meant to be a positive statement at all, but it is just human nature to want to protect ourselves, our assets, and our families. The sooner you realize that the most important person in everyone's life, is themselves, the sooner you can find your "how" to get rich and thrive.

And there is a catch. Just as you might work to bring the right people into your life, those people who want to be there with you in your success, you may also invite the unscrupulous. Money can help bring out the good and bad in people, and there is no reason to pretend that being in the business of getting rich may or may not invite people who are more harmful to your long term success than you would like.

But at least by now, this book stands as a symbol of connecting with someone (the author) who isn't afraid to talk about getting rich and would want riches for you as well! Become the person you would like to have in your life.

And here's something that changed my life…

# 5. No Secrets Here

There is no secret sauce in this book. There are many ways to get rich. So let's examine briefly what the common wisdom flavor of today is.

"Well why do you want to get rich?" some of the success gurus ask. Supposedly it will help you find some deeper meaning that will affect you emotionally and shift the way you view the world.

Although the "why" sets up a great and valid question, it is only a small step in getting you where you initially sought guidance for. and unless you deeply respect the coach that asked you the question and paid a lot of money for them to help you (remember how emotionally attached many people are to money, and what it means for us?), you probably won't make leaps and bounds from it.

Many esteemed thought leaders in wealth and personal development talk about the idea that: "it isn't the money you want, but the feeling you will get from what you can buy with it." They mention things like freedom, happiness, opportunity, excitement, etc… Fair statement and I agree that it is true.

But if you can control your emotions to be happy with and without large quantities of money, why not go after it? If the idea of getting rid of diseases in third world countries seems too far off for you, it might be because you aren't rich enough to fathom how to accomplish that feat.

The mind is powerful, and you can "think big" anytime, and it doesn't matter what your IQ is to get creative. But when you are unsure of how to even attain necessary financial resources, you've got a major roadblock. You're stuck. Let's change that!

And once you realize this concept that a money scarcity approach to life can limit you, then you can start to unlock even more potential within yourself because money itself is more abundant than you might imagine. And when you realize how abundant money is, thinking big and setting massive goals can become easier. And then there are those with the opposite problem of having goals that are way too high and not even remotely realistic for their level of desire, motivation, and skill – but that is for another conversation.

Some people will find that they had an easier time financially, early in their lives when their parents cared for their every need and gave them tremendous love. Some will lack that warm childhood experience but work hard enough, so they have an easier time later in life, and some may fail to realize their potential.

Hopefully you will get to experience the fullness of what life has to offer throughout the entire time. And while you may not need as much money as you think, getting rich and making lots of money can be an exciting prospect.

This book is written to be a part of the dear readers' journey, on your path to becoming rich. Let it be a spark of inspiration – because inspiration is what brought about *Let's Get Rich, QUICK!* in the first place.

The more people who read this book, the more I motivate and help. The more people who get this book, who are inspired to get rich, the more value is added to their lives and even the lives of those affected by the readers of this book. Getting rich together is not about altruism nor is it about greed. This book provides the piece to the puzzle of helping people find success (financial success) in their life, that might be missing from present society.

Whether you are broke, middle class, or just looking to add more to your income, the money will be out there in the world, waiting! And if you are already good at managing your health, mindset, and happiness, knowing that more money is available to you out there and that someone is supportive of you going to get it is a great motivator. Go get that cash!

Great athletes who grew up poor didn't dedicate their lives to accomplishing extraordinary human feats because their parents told them to. They saw sports as a way to get rich and get them and their families out of a tough situation. Sometimes they just needed an escape.

I don't speak for ALL athletes, and while I am not saying all athletes only play to get rich, the large quantities of money likely motivate many players. Why else would people risk getting attacked by 300-pound men in suits of padded armor?

You can analyze the aforementioned scenario of sports players in a variety of ways saying it wasn't the money, it was the family, or it wasn't the family, but it was the teachers, or it wasn't the teachers, but it was the players those kids dreamed about being like on the television screen.

Without the potential for high earnings most athletes may not have chosen to endure their line of work. Professional sports are TOUGH!

If you are looking for practical advice, here it is. Great athletes take massive actions with their bodies, getting pounded and pushing themselves to the peaks of human potential. Business people, artists, and other legends who become rich put their minds to work, and put their best ideas into action!

Don't just think about getting rich hoping and waiting that eventually, some inspiration will fall into your lap making you an overnight success. Expect that it won't until you actively pursue it with great energy. You need to make it happen and picking up this book is a start!

How long does it take to start a business? How long does it take to become an artist? How long does it take to become a doctor? How long does it take to become an athlete?

The decision to do so might take some people 20+ years, or even never because of fear or other life obstacles.

But when you are ready, the decision to do so takes less than a moment's decision, and you can be well on your way.

You can research how to start that corporation, how to paint, how to sing and dance, how to get into medical school, and how to join an amateur sports team (if you missed the opportunity for professional-level play) – and that is an action you can take right now.

How long will it take you to get rich once you decide to do so?

For now, forget trying to find the financial formula or the hot stock tip that will double your money, or whether flipping real estate is the best route for you, or whether you need to find a better niche for your business. You know what they say: "when you stop worrying about and overthinking the problem, the answer sometimes comes."

When you focus on what it will take you to get rich, those answers for those other challenges might come (try it). And for the duration of reading this book, think of getting rich and making a lot of money as the solution.

Now, the question remains: what do you want?

# 6. Seek Success

You come to many realizations about people via coaching calls. One thing I found regularly was that some people *seek failure.* It is an ever-popular belief today that you have to fail before you succeed. And if interpreted literally, you'll find that some people are literally seeking failure.

At first, you might think that it is bizarre. "Who would seek failure? You've got this wrong. Nobody seeks failure, you misunderstood what they meant! They meant that to succeed, there must be some failures along the way!"

That is interpreting what the person said. Let's take it literally for a second a phrase like "I know I have to fail a bit before I find success." The person who says that literally believes they must fail before they succeed!

Things may not work out at your first attempt or first 10,000 attempts, but successful people can overcome those unsuccessful attempts because they are seeking success!

They don't actively look for the ways they might fail at a specific goal or endeavour. They might plan for obstacles that could come along the way, but the point is, stop seeking failure!

Too many people on social media are saying things like "you have to fail before you succeed" or "xyz failed 1000 times before they succeeded!" And I think that causes more people to feel as if they MUST fail before they can find success. Seek success with every mile, while evaluating the potential potholes!

With all of that said, I do not believe people seek failure for the purpose of failing. Let me explain. I think most people inherently seek success, but because of what they have been told, they believe that in order to be successful, there will be some failure along the way, and because of that, they unintentionally seek failure in order to succeed because it "feels good." To put another way, avoid seeking failure in order to find success. You will find plenty of obstacles along the way, that can be virtually guaranteed but see it as an opportunity to grow even further.

While it may be inspirational to learn from the ways others lived prior to success, avoid their mistakes, and model what they did well, believing that you must fail at something along the way to becoming rich will only create obstacles. Now, as you read this sentence, is a good time to focus on success.

Getting rich does not come easily to everyone. For people who have been faced with challenging conditions in life and did not have a solid financial education or did not learn about *money,* you'll have to do an extra step. And that step is to develop an INTENSE MASSIVE desire to get RICH!

How you do that is up to you.
Whether it comes from emotion, maybe even trauma, external or internal motivation, a mentor, or just a fire in your belly, you must find it. This desire has to go beyond just letting the thought flash as you flip through motivational videos.

Here's a quick exercise. Think about a high school student flipping through motivational videos mixed with cat videos who thinks "yea I'd like to be successful and rich! I will be rich one day!" Now think about the intense feelings of someone who grew up in poverty and absolutely hated every aspect of being poor, broke, and hungry, and wore the same shoes from middle school through high school to save money, who also dreams of becoming rich to get out of their situation. Who do you think will have more of the desire to succeed? One merely thinks about it. The other *feels* it.

This is not to say anything negative about the person who is motivated through free internet content. And it is not to say that the same person cannot get rich. By all means, enjoy the richness of entertainment! The important idea to capture is the feeling. Understanding that intense desire – especially if you are not a natural born entrepreneur, businessman/woman, or money maker, can take you far.

Your experiences can fuel you. Whether you seek to get out of a bad situation, or simply move into a much better situation from getting rich, let it be your stored energy. Try to heighten it. You don't need to live in poverty to experience the challenges and pain of poverty to get motivated. Seek success! But understanding the drive to get out of it will definitely help!

And here is where getting rich starts…

# 7. Like Yourself

There is an intensely debated and controversial action you can do regularly to push you along your journey to becoming rich. The premise is simple, and the power of it is hotly discussed. Some call it nothing but procrastination to real action, while others say that this activity is critical to success. And this is as far as we will go into any sort of debate to its' effectiveness.

Affirmations. It is a way to get yourself, and more importantly, your mind to start getting you to take the actions that you must take to become successful. Affirmations help you become the person you wish to become, and to stick to the theme of this book, can help you on your journey to becoming rich.

If you are not happy with yourself, if you do not feel "deserving" of getting rich. If you do not believe you are capable, intelligent, or worthy of becoming rich, chances are you will do things that prove that. Sometimes those negative beliefs are ingrained in us and difficult to get rid of. But at the end of the day, most of those negative beliefs are simply things that you have been telling yourself for far too long, day in and day out. It is time to reverse that, through affirmations.

The successful personal development master Brian Tracy suggests the simple yet powerful affirmation "I like myself."

Evaluate that further. Forget about whether liking yourself is egotistical. If you are far from being egotistical, that is likely not something you have to worry about soon. If you already like yourself, come up with another one yourself. They can range from "I deserve the money I earn" or "I add massive value to the lives of others" to "I believe in myself and I know others do too."

Spending the time to tell yourself out loud, that you like yourself (or any positive affirmation for that matter), will eventually have its' positive effect. It sounds like nonsense but think about the alternative: telling yourself that you do not like yourself.

When you start to tell yourself and believe positive things, eventually those things will start to become apparent. Apparent being the key word, and apparent does not mean magically appear out of thin air.

This may be the hardest chapter to develop any sort of mastery over. Making more money is as simple as getting a better job. Coming up with great ideas is as simple as putting in the work or reading lots of books. But you have to live with yourself and your mind every single day. Be the person you would like to have around you. It can be difficult to help others when you have not helped yourself.

The goal is to become someone that other's like and would wish success on. *Let's Get Rich, QUICK!* is about going the distance. Whether you want to get rich for the sake of being rich or get rich for the sake of owning a mega-yacht or get rich for the sake of pursuing an art or contributing to a philanthropy, let's make it happen! I want you to get there! And you enjoying your individual company along the way will allow you to reap rewards.

As feel good as this chapter is, balance is still needed. Affirmations are so powerful that they can create delusions. Delusions are not suggesting that ones goals are too high, or that a significant boost in confidence or passion is unhealthy.

The point is to take affirmations seriously. You can use it to tell yourself you are the Almighty King of the World, but when your real-world stops adding up to that, problems can arise. Getting rich is much more likely to happen than being an Almighty King of the World. You want to get rich and be happy while doing it.

Prepare yourself for what is to come, because it might come quicker than you expect…

# 8. Advance, Not Stagnate

The world works based on numerous scientific laws and theories. The concepts also carry over into the world of money.

Ever notice how people who are fit and in shape consistently go to the gym day in and day out, year in and year out? Ever notice that "objects that in motion, stay in motion in the same direction unless acted upon by an unbalanced force?"

To get rich, some of us have to persist longer than others. When you get into motion and start building momentum, you will stay in motion unless you come across some force that takes you off balance. When people think of others' "failures" or taking "many attempts" before becoming successful, it is that very force that takes those people off balance that most of us are witnessing.

The person who succeeds and finds riches is the one that continues getting back into motion. If you let a seemingly immovable force stop you, you will stagnate.

When the unstoppable force meets the immovable force, it doesn't matter what happens, but one thing for sure, the energy from that collision must go somewhere! And if we take a fictional scenario of a near-unstoppable villain meeting an immovable object, if the fictional villain stops and stares at the immovable object indefinitely, he will starve! And when you stagnate, you are shrinking.

There is arguably no such thing as standing still because time is always moving, and the world is constantly transitioning around you. You are either moving forward or backward.

You can't get richer than you are doing the same thing you are doing or just holding on to money. Your money becomes worth less (not necessarily worthless) every moment through inflation. Without going into complex economic analysis, the fact is, when it comes to money, if it is not working, it is decreasing in the big picture of things. And obviously the challenge comes down to getting your money to work in the most effective way possible.

Here is a practical way to start constantly advancing instead of stagnating: focus on seeking solutions that doesn't involve talking to a banker or financial advisor.

Let us take, for example, the decision of whether or not to leave a company to pursue an entrepreneurial dream that you've been working on. In both situations, you are either sitting, laying down, or standing in thought about the scenario at different moments in time.

Now, if you see the entire situation of leaving the company and becoming an entrepreneur as one major problem, thinking about nothing but every problem as dreadful and frightening, the decision to say yes to the opportunity will be very difficult.

Now, if you see the entire situation as a massive opportunity with massive potential and think more about the solutions to the challenges you might face, you are more likely to get yourself into action, as opposed to "thinking on" the decision. This scenario can be analogized for just about any situation out there.

Advance through the development of solutions so that you *can* get where you want to go. This book is a symbol that we are both on a common journey to get rich. And I may have the opportunity to meet just a portion of the people who read this book. But regardless of whether we meet or ever do business together, few of any people will ever care about your success more than you. And if they do, it would not be sustainable as they would need to literally live with and support you every waking moment, and even be in your mind.

Also important, trying to get rich based on the common wisdom of the ages (save your pennies, leave your money with a banker, and let your money grow over 50 years to have barely enough for a fully enjoyable retirement) is outdated. Work on making your desire to advance and get rich so intense that you get there *quickly.* We want to be able to enjoy it, after all.

*Let's Get Rich, QUICK!* in our own unique way.

# 9. Why Money?

A premise for this book is that making a ton of money is just as valid to being happy and living a fulfilled life as any other purpose or passion out there. Over time, making a lot of money has somehow developed a negative connotation.

Money without purpose, ethics, and integrity could be very terrible and wasteful. Purpose and passion without money can lead to unfulfilled hopes, technologies, medicines, art, shattered dreams and more…

So comes the question, passion, or money? If you follow your passion will the money come? Let's reverse that! If you follow the money, will you find the time to pursue your passion? *Let's Get Rich, QUICK!*

Let me ask you. Why does seeking money have to be any better or worse than seeking a purpose or passion? Forget about what the "coaches" say (and nothing against coaches – I very much appreciate the coaches I've had) and forget the cautionary messages from Hollywood movies about the challenges of getting rich for a moment. Be aware, but don't get stuck.

People have failed trying to get rich, but people also have, for centuries, failed trying to find their purpose, or to find enough time to do things they are passionate about or love.

People have wasted time doing things they don't care about, hoping that they will get "rich enough" after 50 years. People have also wasted time getting rich when all they wanted was to do spiritual work or go fishing.

Another common argument against getting rich is that money does not give strength and that if you tie too much of your "meaning" to getting rich, and lose it all, you may never get it back. Going back to the chapter on Seeking success, those people are already planning to potentially lose it all?

While it is far from impossible to lose all of your money on a bad investment or failed business, there are two things wrong with these assumptions. One is that obviously, they imagine what happens if you fail. The second one is that the logic assumes that external factors like money do not create any drive. But remember, most people have deep emotional attachments and beliefs about money! Just like they have deep emotional attachments to their pets, family heirlooms, cars, friends, and more. Maybe not all in the same way, but the point is, "so what if an external factor like money helps someone find more strength in what they do? *Let's Get Rich, QUICK!* Why not?

This book is written for people who want to get rich. It's fine, it is ok to admit you want to get rich! If you feel uncomfortable telling others, that's ok too, but make sure that you at least set the goal for yourself! And you might have trouble doing that.

Society has ingrained in many of us that there might be something wrong with getting rich. And a few people might even have a negative experience with some rich people, just as they might have had a bad experience with some people who are not so rich.

Do not let a few small samples bother you! There are millions of millionaires in the world! You would be unfairly judging if you thought all of them are the same! You are hurting only yourself by doing so.

Money gets you a lot of things, let's not beat around the bush about that. Whether you decide to buy your private jet, island, or travel the world in style or start a world-improving company, money gives you the options to choose! Now obviously, if you don't work to keep and create more income, it will eventually go away. But the fact is, getting rich is freedom.

Forget about whether paparazzi will follow you or whether a news article will be shared about you. If you are concerned about that, it might be better to stay low-key rich.

If you get ultra-rich, that might be a bit tougher, but dealing with paparazzi might be a bit more interesting than being stuck trying to figure out how you are going to save for your kids college, if and when you can eventually afford to have kids. Money can represent freedom and a way out of a tough situation.

Don't get bogged down by the famous idea "more money more problems." You are always going to have problems in life. More money will just give you different decisions that will create learning experiences.

If you've never needed an accountant, or financial advisor, and feel against having one while broke (and they probably wouldn't want to work with you either), you may need to decide on one, or even an entire firm to help manage your money. Figuring out how to pay back that $500 loan from a friend is not that different from figuring out how you are going to pay that company to maintain your yacht.

Evaluate things in scale. Would you rather struggle to figure out $500 or $100,000? The $100,000 sounds tough when you don't have or know how to get it, but for someone rich enough, they will figure it out. You might even find that the more "expensive" decisions even take less time and energy when you get there.

Think of it as being great to have big problems!

Would you rather have a boss beating down your door to get more performance out of you for the same basic salary? Or would you rather have successful people coming to you for advice? Would you rather try to figure out how to make your next million or stuck wondering how you are going to pay your overdue bills?

Would you rather figure out how your major contribution and attendance at a charity will have a massive impact, or would you rather be struggling to figure out if you will have time between your two jobs to do non-profit volunteering?

Being rich does not make people suddenly immune to the challenges of being human and the emotions that go with it. The media does a great job of magnifying the things that go wrong with the rich, though. But for every rich person who has a challenge like a child who has a bad case of "affluenza" – there is another child who is less fortunate, who has another problem.

When the value of money and what it represents is misunderstood, it is a source of problems that are worth addressing. But why let what the news and movies say about rich people stop you? Being rich is not so bad.

Even Scrooge found massive happiness after he had a change of heart, but there would not have been that option for him if he was destitute. The message there is that it isn't money that is bad. Getting rich is not bad. It is the application and management of the resources that may bring about positive or negative impacts on the world of those around you.

How much time do you spend on the small things? I'm not talking about small things that you might be passionate about. I'm not evaluating whether what you do is "big or small."

Only that there are things in your life Yes, small things add up, and they matter in some cases. Being detail-oriented is a valuable skill to help you get rich. But the bigger (scale-wise) your problems are, the better position you might be in.

Money is one of the most important human-made resources on Earth. Relationships, empathy, community, purpose, and all those things are important in life, but without money, we'd be back to trading stones and cows – do you know how to raise, breed, and sell a cow?

The question remains then, when do you want to get rich? Better sooner and quicker than later, right? That's what we are here for. *Let's Get Rich, QUICK!*

# 10. Let's Do Mathematics

Regardless of your current age in life, now is a great time to do some math to think about what you need to get rich before you can no longer enjoy it to the fullest potential. If you are in a government job, soon retiring and want to live the rest of those days comfortably, more power to you.

The concept of getting rich quick is not about "overnight success." It is about lighting a fire under you to not spend the next 20+ years of your life, hoping to get rich. Get there sooner rather than later.

According to a simple compound interest calculator I used, if you already saved $200,000, add an extra $10,000 each year, and you grow that for 20 years, with an interest rate of 5%, you will only have a future value of $877,852.06. You will not have a million in the bank. Saving an extra $10k per year will be difficult, depending on the situation.

Hopefully, by that time, you'll have other assets that will get you there, but if you retire, you will need to keep working as you live on about $40k+ per year through retirement depending on your expenses.

No need to overanalyze the math here, you can play with numbers all day on calculators you can find online. And you'll probably even realize the incredible challenge it might to even be able to work with those numbers in today's job economy.

Now consider this alternative.

You spend a solid two years (usually requires more – and I'm talking about education beyond just college) learning everything you can about making money, entrepreneurship, growing in your career, developing technology, and becoming an artist even (while working a regular job. Then you spend a year developing a business idea (it probably requires much less). Spend the next five years building the company into a multi-hundred thousand, or multi-million dollar business. You can potentially become a millionaire in less than ten years.

What happens if you don't want to be an entrepreneur or artist? You can dedicate the same amount of time to a career or job and demonstrate tremendous skill. But with the politics involved, and constant changes in the economy today, that route is fraught with tremendous risk as well.

*Let's Get Rich, QUICK!* is not another book to make you scared about the economy. Fear disempowers. If you are scared about what could happen if you lose your job, you'll be more likely to stick to a crappy one! But if you recognize the opportunities available in today's economy, you may be more likely to jump on the abundance of opportunities around you! It is the difference between overcoming fear and uncertainty which is very difficult and making an exciting decision, and taking action that will separate who you want to become from who you are today.

Let's do more math to get you excited. Suspend the idea that you have a job for a second where you work for a week, and you get X amount of dollars. A job will not get you rich unless you effectively get into a successful startup with some stock options, at which case, you have taken ownership.

What does it take to make $1000? You have to sell 1 product or service for $1000, 10 for $100, or 100 for $10.

What does it take to make $1,000,000? In terms of products and services you have to sell:

1 product or service for $1,000,000 (paintings, a business, a house, antique, something incredibly rare)

10 for $100,000 (luxury car, boat, apartment unit, consulting, luxury memberships)

100 for $10,000 (high ticket events, luxury rental units, furniture, remodeling services)

1000 for $1,000 (consulting, smaller rare items, art, phones, exercise equipment)

10,000 for $100 (internet software, subscriptions, clothing, accessories, etc…)

You don't need complex math to get started on getting rich.
There are people called "quants" whose sole purpose is to do math and evaluate investments based on numbers, and you can make a lot of money solving complex math problems for companies.

And yes having a good grasp of financial principles, economics, and accounting is very useful. But understanding what to do to make money is simple: you must sell products or services. Simple math and multiplication easily done by a calculator can get you started on figuring out what you need to be rich!

There is something to be said about the man or woman who stays at a company for 40+ years, takes the reigns as the obvious choice for CEO, and becomes very rich making 10s of millions per year. Chances are they started reaching a level considered "rich" before that C-Suite. And if that is how you want to get rich, more power to you.

Getting rich quick in 5-10 years (or less) based on a few good business ideas could even lead to stagnation. Not everyone starts a business and becomes massively rich.

In fact, most entrepreneurs start a business only to find it is more stressful than their previous jobs with relatively equal levels of pay, but at least they are the boss of their destiny. This is based on articles I've read online.

But turnover in corporations are more common than ever, and there are millions of people who wanted to get rich working at a company but never reached that C-Suite. But at the top, you can still make great money. A brief note here. It may not be money alone that drives people to the top of the Fortune 500 executive suites, but isn't it interesting that they all tend to have a lot of it?

A final mathematical idea if you are a numbers person. You don't even need to know basic math to realize this. But strictly speaking of numbers, there are more people on the planet earth than has ever lived! There are more customers and more products than ever before. There are even more ways to make money with just a single smartphone. Now the opportunities to make massive dollars are may not be as simple as logging onto the highest paying ride share app. But beyond that, the tools to create, produce and develop instead of just consuming are in the palm of your hands!

The big challenge comes from having enough management of yourself and your mind backed with a massive desire to get rich! Your ideas, mentors, professional relationships, and money will come when you sow the seeds, and it all starts first with wanting to get rich!

# 11. Say No to Mediocre

What keeps people from becoming incredibly rich or incredibly successful in life? It would be near impossible to track every rag to riches story down to the finest detail although there are lots of people putting in the work to know what separates the rich and successful from those who are not.

Is the answer a great idea? Maybe early life circumstances? Perhaps it's getting lucky on Wall Street? One single moment where they were "discovered"? You can overthink it and analyze what everyone else has that you do not have.

But one thing that keeps people moving is that they do not settle! I have spoken to numerous people who inherited a family business that does well, and when asked what they want to do to grow the business, they say something along the lines of "there is a lot of opportunities! I know this company can do 10-20%+ more." But when asked about the actions they want to take on to grow the business, they settle into a state of comfort and risk aversion.

Now those scenarios have been few and far between, but they exist. Businesses and people stop growing because they feel as if they've achieved their limits, or they want just to be comfortable and relax after many years of hard work. All that is fair, and they earned it when they got rich!

But for those reading who have not reached the point of becoming financially rich, and those who have not even accepted that it is possible yet, and everyone in between and around, you can't get there unless you've decided that you can. You need to believe that you will get there, and in many cases, some would say you even have to believe you are already there, and that it is your fate!

Look, I'm not here to judge. If you want to live an average or mediocre life, go for it as long as you are happy. But if you have ever wanted to experience life as those do with a lot of money, the biggest obstacle in your way is yourself.

How difficult is it really, to:
Make videos if you want to be a producer, director, artist, etc…? Use your phone.
Get an idea for a toy developed? Look up, "toy manufacturers."
Find a job that pays even a little bit more? Job search websites.
Text a friend with a business idea? Hello.
Think in silence about your next big idea? Bedroom or living room and a pen and paper.
Come up with a better and more effective way to do something? Send your comments into a customer support department or email the executives directly from their website.
Engage with a leading executive and thought leader on social media? Just make an account and come up with something worth engaging for.

Buy a high-quality consumer-level microphone for your podcasting career? Save up $200.

Dedicate your time to studying Quantum Physics? Go to the library – how do you plan on getting rich with that? If you just love Quantum Physics, keep yourself happy!

Work in the industry of your dreams? Make a list of companies and contacts in that industry.

Be around successful and wealthy people? Move to an area or hang around a spot where those types of people regularly visit.

While every opportunity that we go for may not work out perfectly, the fact is, most of what stops us is ourselves. When other people tell us "no" or "don't do that" or "you're not good enough," there are those who take up the challenge, and those who succumb. Those people might even be friends and family with good intentions of "protecting you" but protecting you does not help you prosper if it is not done the right way.

Decide that you want to get rich and that getting rich is possible for you. Find the people who are there to either help, support, or do business with you. Although it may not be easy, forget about those negative beliefs you've held about becoming rich, or the rich.

And if you choose not to, you have two options. Either you can coast through life in your negative state of mind and possibly never experiencing the riches that you deserve, or you can do your best to get rich so you can prove those negative stereotypes wrong about what it means to be rich!

You've heard it before, and I'll repeat it. Getting rich does not happen overnight, but it can happen quickly. Maybe even quicker than you originally planned.

When people worked in small rural towns before the internet, it is understandable that it would be difficult to fathom how you could get rich. Imagine living in a town of fewer than 500 people, and everyone has their own "family business" of farming, owning a small convenience store, or some other form of service.

Without computers and the internet, you only had access to that very limited group of 500 people! You may not have recognized the massive opportunities to sell products or connect with manufacturers in other parts of the world. Travel took a tremendous amount of time, and communication was way more difficult. And maybe that handful of very wealthy town leaders, say the top 1% or 5 of them had a lot of money that you could seek for financing. But today, a large portion of the world is at your fingertips with the internet!

Take time to psyche yourself up if you have to. If you feel embarrassed getting yourself into an energized state to take on a work task, then can you expect that you will be able to do so when opportunity knocks? Aim high! There is nothing new to be said about reaching even higher than you think because when you do, your success will land somewhere further than if you aimed low.

It is almost justifiable why people in those days did not strive for more, they had less opportunity. But today, you can become rich by making lip-syncing videos on social media and doing pranks in public!

Almost unfathomable back in the day. And even in those days, sure there were technological limitations, but the lack of desire to leave the town, or to connect with the town's bankers, or to seek locations of greater opportunity were their own. Imagine only having a potential client base of 500 people!

Either you need to sell them a lot of products, or a lot of them have to get rich enough to afford a high-end service from you.

Accepting a mediocre state of living will get you exactly what you want. But taking on exceptional tasks, and having the desire to live an exceptional life will likely get you even beyond your imagination.

I want to briefly touch on imagination right now. Some people will say "well I have an imagination, I want to imagine a trillion dollars in my bank account by tomorrow, and that doesn't happen!" Or "time travel doesn't exist, and I could imagine all I want, but I won't develop time travel in my lifetime to get rich!"

My argument is, yes you very well could! Even if your idea is not physically and technologically possible, if you truly care enough about time travel, you could probably come up with a worthy movie idea or book to write about time traveling by the morning! You could probably even develop theories around time travel, post them on a streaming video platform, build lectures around it, and still get rich!

*Let's Get Rich, QUICK!* is not about trying to do the physically impossible. It is about recognizing the opportunities and the potential around you! And it is about getting rich! If you want to get rich, stop worrying about what is "not possible." Think about what you can achieve. Regardless of where you are right now, rich trying to get richer or poor trying to get massively rich, say no to mediocre.

Now that you're unstuck from your own thoughts…

# 12. Get Inspired

Napoleon Hill, author of *Think and Grow Rich,* says that the drive for sex is arguably the number one motivator for a person's success. Napoleon Hill specifically stated men, but chalk that up to the era he wrote in, and the way society was. But women are doing great in business today and at getting rich!

Whether you are inspired by the opposite sex, the same sex, great leaders, stories, movies, books, seminars, philosophy, meditation, or even yourself, it would be beneficial to be on the search for it if you want to get rich!

Many artists did their best work either while inspired by a muse, or after a difficult break-up. Many business people are driven into action after a bad business deal, or even being pushed to achieve greater success by their managers. While it would be great to have "positive inspirations" where there was "no loss" for us, those negative inspirations that give us a bit of pain could help you get where you want to go.

Real quickly, this does not mean you necessarily need to experience a negative inspiration to get into action to becoming rich. If you actively seek that, you might be acting on the wrong ideas. For that, realize that there will be plenty of obstacles along the way that can cause those negative inspirations even without your having to find them.

Maybe this book inspires you to get rich. Maybe getting rich doesn't even inspire you, but everything you can do with more money does! Maybe saving the planet, animals, dogs, souls, bad neighborhoods, or something else inspires you. You don't necessarily need to get rich to start doing your part. But if you want to have an even bigger impact in any of those areas, you have to have a desire to get rich!

Now some people say that if you start doing what it is you ultimately want to be doing at some point, you will be happy, and money won't matter.

For example, if you have dreams of becoming a successful painter, or opera singer, or philanthropist, that all you need to do is get started on it, and "money will come," and you will be happy while you're pursuing your passion. But the problem with that is, most people who seek only "passion" end up forgetting about money!

Forgetting about money is a good thing when you are making enough to get by while doing what you love. But when you are struggling, and you lack a desire for money, you won't ask for it, or you don't have to skill to.

Take, for example, the budding artist who does not ask for what his painting is worth. Or the entrepreneur who undersells his services. Or the business manager who believes they can build a great team on "motivation alone" because he has to cut costs – when, in fact the business manager might probably be more effective trying to ask for more money for his team from his leadership.

Most of us have a start-up phase in life where we are not getting fully what we are worth. Some of us stay there for far too long. Some industries even expect you to intern for minimum wage, take a low salary (or commissions only), or even work for free to build your name for yourself. Fine, but remember to keep the end goal in mind.

And here is something about the desire to get rich. For those that want it badly enough, you will likely eventually get there. And by that time, when you reach a level of wealth and financial success you are happy with, this book will no longer be valid in your life.

You'll be on to bigger and better things. You may seek more purpose, or focus your attention not so much on getting richer but pursuing your passions. And when you get there, definitely check in and see if you are settling.

Getting inspired is simple. Simply think about the things that stimulate your mind. Think to the past of the things that you seemed to lose time doing (in a good way). Maybe it's gaming, reading, writing, playing chess, business meetings, teaching your little brother the ropes of life, fishing, meditation, and anything else.

Notice what those experiences felt like, and

that might be your key to finding inspiration. Most inspiration comes from external sources. In order to build the light bulb, Thomas Edison had to be inspired by a combination of glass, chemistry, physics, and electricity.

To write Harry Potter, J.K. Rowling had to be inspired by her children, people, fantasy, and a combination of things that got her into writing. To create Disney, Marvel, Apple, Wal-Mart, Amazon, and more, their founders (although brilliant and hardworking) likely found inspiration from external sources.

Another way to get inspiration is to change up what it is you do! Visit another city, write another article, start another job, or make a new inspirational video. Get uncomfortable.

Come up with an idea so big you wouldn't feel comfortable taking on. Eventually, you'll be so inspired, and thinking so big, and so motivated to get rich, that your performance at a six will seem like a 10 to others.

A lot of getting rich has to do with perception as well. The reason why some people get so rich and successful isn't just because they are brilliant beyond reach. It is because they have dedicated their lives to becoming who they are, and those valuable habits, attitudes, beliefs, relationships and more.

By the time they reach a level of wealth and success, they seem extraordinary! Yet at the end of the day, they are still people with insecurities, challenges, fears, and worries. But they seem extraordinary because the average person proceeds through life at an average pace, and have not developed those same necessary habits, attitudes, beliefs, relationships, and more.

Quicker than it takes for a rock to fall from your hand to hit the floor, your favorite music artist or athlete can hit a 6 out of 10 on their scale of high performance and energy – which to the average performer or athlete might see as off the charts! They have conditioned themselves to perform at a high level at any necessary moment so high, and so often, that to the untrained person, they seem out of this world.

By now, from reading this book, you are probably motivated and energized to get rich. That has been the goal here. By becoming aware of the possibilities available for you and finding the energy from within yourself to realize you can get there, you have taken a massive leap. Before we wrap up this book, let's talk about some final actions.

# 13. Spread the Wealth

After some research, I found that some things that keep people broke are hoarding (of money), fear, and having a broke mindset. People horde because of loss of something (as opposed to the giving away for a beneficial cause). They might fear they may never get something of equal value back. I'm not talking about hoarding in a home where an entire house is filled with every item collected over the past 30 years, but specifically the hoarding of money.

Although the all famous story of Scrooge and hoarding enormous piles of money in his vault paints our image of greedy unhappy money hoarder, you have to ask yourself, what did Scrooge even do for work? While there are a lot of stingy people out there, the wealthiest of them all is likely very giving. And to that end, I say we should all learn a little bit from them!

The common assumption here is that the rich only give to non-profit causes because it is beneficial for them when it comes time for taxes. So what? Everyone has the same opportunity to work with a good accountant to account for charitable donations, whether they are to your local religious organization, a non-profit to help veterans, or even books to your local library. And we are all born with the primary skill you need to become rich, which is the ability to think effectively – and it is possible to hone it.

Going back to Scrooge, who is painted as a rich loner is so deceiving. This similar character is even portrayed in the movie *There Will Be Blood*. But the reason massively rich people get rich and powerful, is because the people around them, that work for them or with them, also become rich! Maybe the front-line entry-level employees don't always have the opportunity to get rich, quick. But over time, simply by working on the right projects, and delivering valuable work, they eventually position themselves to become rich.

And more and more, every day, the very rich are sharing their stories so that others can learn from their success. I'm not just talking about popular motivational quotes. I'm talking about step by step books and trails that explain how to: invest, flip houses, uncover new ideas, market a brand, get rich whether you are a man or woman, build engines, and stories about the moments that changed their lives. Some are even setting plans to donate their fortunes to good causes when the time is right.

I am sure there are some very rich people who have done nothing but unethical acts, hoard their cash and have 0 desire to share any of it. They live up to the stereotype of greedy rich people. Wanting to get rich or even richer is not greedy. Being greedy is greedy.

The idea here is to spread the wealth, whether it be invaluable knowledge, charitable causes, or developing a product that will massively improve people's lives.

If you have a good idea, put it into action! If you plan on donating to a charity 40 years from now, when you are a millionaire, you are doing it wrong. Donate today! If you have an experience or story to share, don't wait another 30 years when you are 1,000 times further than you are today, do it today! There probably will be tomorrow, and that is how we live our lives – "I'll do it tomorrow." But the attitude that will set us up for success is "what can I do right now?"

Decide that you will become rich now. Take action based on that – do you have a bill to pay? Pay yourself, then pay your bill. Do you have a business contact you've been meaning to call? Give them a call! Do you have an idea you've been wanting to research? Open your search engine and search. Have you been wanting to write a book, make videos, plan a seminar, get a new job, ask your boss for a raise, learn about real estate/stocks/commodities, etc..? Get into action!

There will be countless other books out there to help you find happiness. So let's make sure we do everything we can do make the most of our potential. And many times, either riches will come with that, or we need to develop an understanding of how to get rich so that we execute on our plans.

# Conclusion

Get rich enough to buy your own island, construct a massive hotel, and fly around on a private jet. Or you can get rich enough to just retire early and play golf. Either way, you'll need some urgency.

Time will not wait for you to get rich. The common wisdom about aiming to get rich in 20-40 years is ultimately there to help you realize that getting rich and having at least $1million in the bank is very possible with very little risk.

But the world is changing, and there is more uncertainty and risk with what used to be the safe path. And there are more opportunities to get rich in less than 10 years than ever before! It is time to decide that you want it and start your plan and course of action.

Whether rich means just enough to keep food on the table, and a roof over your head, or being a major shareholder and founder of a business worth billions, it all starts with the decision to get there.

And along that journey, you will face exciting times and challenging times. You may find that getting rich brings happiness, and maybe it doesn't. You will have lovers, and haters. Whatever happens, don't give up before you even start! Set your intentions, realize the urgency, and get into action!

# About the Author

Emmett Ferguson has an MBA from the Jack Welch Management Institute.

He writes on the topics of personal and professional development.

He is also the author of *Don't Be Selfish, Share Your Art with the World*, *The Power of Starting Today*, and *20 Scientific Habits to Confident Cold Call*.

Emmett spent many years in customer-facing positions including B2C, B2B, prospecting, cold calling, account management, and even door to door sales.

He also has experience as a coaching practice for personal development and continues to study sales, marketing, and business growth strategies relevant today.

Follow him on LinkedIn, Facebook, Twitter, and Instagram @mindsetferg

www.ingramcontent.com/pod-product-compliance
Lightning Source LLC
Chambersburg PA
CBHW070455220526
45466CB00004B/1843